MOMMY MUST BE A FOUNTAIN OF FEATHERS

Kim Hyesoon
translated by Don Mee Choi

ACTION BOOKS / NOTRE DAME IN / 2008

Action Books is deeply grateful to the Korea Literature Translation Institute (KLTI).
Their generous grants made possible the translation of these poems
and the publication of this book.

Action Books gratefully acknowledges the generosity
of the University of Notre Dame in supporting our mission
as a press.

ACTION BOOKS

Department of English
University of Notre Dame
356 O'Shaughnessy Hall
Notre Dame, IN 46556-5639

WWW.ACTIONBOOKS.ORG

EDITORS: Joyelle McSweeney & Johannes Göransson
ART DIRECTION: Jesper Göransson & Eli Queen
ASSISTANT EDITOR: Kristina Sigler
WEB DESIGN AND EDITORIAL: John Dermot Wood
EDITORIAL ASSISTANT: Christine Nguyen

FIRST EDITION

CONTENTS

Part Two

Part Three

TRANSLATOR'S INTRODUCTION

I MET KIM HYESOON for the first time in Seoul, in 2001. We decided by phone to meet at a Starbucks in an arts district called Hyehwadong, so we could find each other easily. She told me she had glasses and short hair. I did not say I also wore glasses. Somehow it felt important that I find her first the way I had found her poetry while I was searching, actually floundering about, for the right kind of bridge that would allow a return to my first home, South Korea, which I had left in 1972. Kim insisted on treating me to lunch at a noodle shop that she and her husband, the renowned playwright Yi Kang-baek, often went to. I ordered a hot noodle soup that came with elaborate side dishes. As soon as Kim was done with her simple cold noodles, words began to pour out of her. She began to tell me how she had met her husband soon after the military coup led by General Chun Doo Hwan in 1980. Many consider the 1980s worse than the previous two decades of dictatorship under President Park Chung Hee, a chapter which came to an end with Park's assassination by his intelligence officer in 1979. As soon as General Chun came into power, all publications were even more rigorously censored. Newspapers hit the stands with whole sections blacked out with ink. Kim Hyesoon had just graduated and was working as an editor for a publishing house. She was in charge of Yi's play called *Kaeppul* [Dog's Horns], a piece considered the quintessential expression of life under the military dictatorship of the 1970s. Submitted to state censors, Yi's play came back to Kim completely blackened except for the title and Yi's name. It is from such blackened space that, I believe, Kim Hyesoon's poetry emerges.

Prior to the early twentieth century, Korean women's poetry existed primarily within the oral tradition. Women were restricted from learning the written language, which was then classical Chinese, except for Korean script, *hangŭl*, a writing system promulgated in 1446 for women and commoners. The written literary realm was dominated by men and still is. Pioneer women poets of the 1920s published their work publicly for the first time and displayed in their poems acute awareness of Korean patriarchy and oppressive women's conditions. Yet Korean women's poetry since then has been characterized by a language of passivity and contemplation that was predefined by the literary establishment. It wasn't till the late 1970s that a women's poetry energized by feminist consciousness and innovation began to challenge the status quo. And Kim Hyesoon is one of the few women poets, along with Ch'oe Sŭng-ja, to arrive on the scene with a stunning language of resistance to the prescribed literary conventions for women. For Kim the blackened space is the realm in which women from the traditional era expressed their social conditions.

This realm has long been traveled by women represented in Korean shaman narratives, muga. In her book of essays called *Yŏsŏngi kŭrŭl ssŭndanŭn kŏtsŭn*[1] [To Write as a Woman], Kim explores a *muga* called *"Paridaegi"* [The Abandoned] also known as *"Parigongju"* [Princess Abandoned] who goes on an arduous journey through the realm of the dead—hell—in search of medicinal water for her ailing parents who had abandoned her at birth for being their seventh daughter—one daughter too many. After saving her parents, *Paridaegi* becomes a spirit and guides the dead to another realm. For Kim the blackened space is not only the space of oppression but also a place where a woman redefines herself, retranslates herself. Therefore, I see Kim's poetry as poetry of translation. And in my role as a translator, I guide Kim's translated blackened self to another place, another language, across a bridge forged by history—the history of the U.S. presence in Korea since 1945. The U.S. presence translates into about one hundred U.S. military bases and installations in South Korea, a land that is only one fourth the size of California. Its 1997 economic crisis led to IMF (International Monetary Fund) structural adjustment loans and has made South Korea vulnerable to further control and regulations, the most recent being the Korea-U.S. (KORUS) Free Trade Agreement, which, if enacted, would devastate the already struggling South Korean farmers. Despite South Korea's rise to relative prosperity as the world's eleventh largest economy, the degree to which it remains culturally and politically subservient to the U.S. cannot be underestimated. I need to state the obvious: South Korea is a neocolony.

Kim Hyesoon and I met again, but this time in the U.S. when she was invited to give a reading at Smith College in 2003. We shared a hotel room, and since we thought that there was nothing to do in Northampton, which Kim referred to as "heaven," we came back to our room. In bed, Kim started to read her poems aloud to me. It struck me that all the poems had rats in them. A few months later, I began translating what I thought of as Kim's "rat poems," which later Susan Schultz, the editor of Tinfish, published as a "rat chapbook" called *When the Plug Get Unplugged* in 2005. It made total sense to me that Kim's blackened realm would be populated by rats copulating, raising a family, mommy rats gnawing at baby rats, surviving hell. Kim translates hell, as a daughter of a neocolony, and I translate her translated hell as a daughter from the neocolony—two daughters too many. In *To Write as a Woman,* Kim reveals hell as a "place of death within life.... the place *Paridaegi* goes to, the place she travels to via death is a feminine space of creation. It is *hyŏnbin.*" She explains *hyŏn* as "closed eyes therefore everything is black" and *bin* as "a signifier for a woman's reproductive organs, a mouth of a lock, a valley, a mountain spring.... Inside this dark womb the possibility of all life is held. At that place patriarchy, the male-centered thing breaks, the universality of all things breaks." Clearly, this is a place of women's chorus, not KORUS.

Kim translates *hyŏnbin,* the blackened realm within the hierarchies of KORUS. Elfried Jelinek says in her essay, "Trans - lation (- portation),"[2] : "I gaze into the certain, because the authors I translate knew what makes the clockwork of society tick.... And this knowledge about hierarchies and rules drops like a net, like a transparency (transparent!) or banner (bann-her!) over the staged asylum into which we theatergoers are allowed to peer, and which makes it once more into an orderly middle class dwelling, where everything has its place, exactly where it belongs." Kim's banner acts like a mirror, reflecting back to us the broken hierarchies of KORUS: heavy Fathers, Father's enemy, troops, historical events, and Father's collapsed pink department store and janitors. Kim's rats and dogs roam about Father's broken landscape. Everything breaks and everything gets eaten as "Seoul eats and shits through the same door" from "the desire of the abandoned woman wanting to raise an abandoned woman" which Kim says "leads to the creation of a feminine text. No, it is the text that moves toward desire." Kim's text is horizontal like the blackened realm towards which *Paridaegi* travels. *Paridaegi* moves horizontally across space, from life to death. Therefore Kim notes that we see the same things that we see in everyday life in death, as well, including women's daily work. We see mommy washing dishes, making feather breakfasts. And we see a mommy rat and daddy rat and a stranded North Korean submarine that has crossed over to the South and the soldiers who shoot themselves in a suicide pact. Fattened by desire, Kim's rats scurry horizontally in and out of the KORUS of Seoul and chorus of hell. They survive.

Kim Hyesoon and I met once again in 2006 at the American Literary Translators Association's annual conference in Seattle. She was asked by someone what she thought of my translation of her poetry. She answered, "It is like meeting someone like myself." Her astute answer implied to me that she thought beyond the well-known and accepted expectation, a faithful or absolute translation, a notion Paul Ricoeur[3] refers to as "a fantasy of perfect translation." Instead he argues for the "loss of linguistic absolute" and proposes the notion of "linguistic hospitality…the pleasure of dwelling in the other's language is balanced by the pleasure of receiving the foreign word at home, in one's own welcoming house." Kim understands her translated text as an entirely separate thing, a different house that reminds her of her own house. And because I used to dwell in the same house as Kim, the words or texts that I receive into my new house, distant from the house of my childhood, are not foreign. Therefore, for me "linguistic hospitality" involves first returning to my childhood home, then departing to my current dwelling in the U.S. It is an act of linguistic return, and, hence, a perpetual farewell. As in Kim's own translation of the blackened realm where two different realities are accessed from the same horizontal plane, the English translation of Kim's poetry also exists on the same plane as the original poem, but it is made of a different linguistic and cultural mirror. When two such mirrors meet, twoness is forged and become inseparable. My translation is born from the twoness—the chorus of mirrors, mirrors against KORUS.

DON MEE CHOI
SEATTLE, WA
OCTOBER, 2007

1 Kim Hyesoon. *Yŏsŏngi kŭrŭl ssŭndanŭn kŏtsŭn* [To Write as a Woman]. Seoul: Munhakdongne, 2002.

2 Jelinek, Elfriede. "Trans – lation (- portation)." Trans. Janet Swaffar *Elfriede Jelinek: Framed by Language*. Ed. Jorun B. Johns and Katherine Arens. Riverside, CA: Ariadne Press. 1-7.

3 Ricoeur, Paul. *On Translation*. Trans. Eileen Brennan. London and New York: Routledge, 2006.

PART ONE

Cut my hair short again
I don't want to pull out
the names etched onto my hair that grows daily
As rain fell, garbage bins from the 2nd, 3rd, 4th floor
must have been turned upside down
Hair fell profusely
I kissed in a place where garbage came down like rain
I kissed where I vomited all night long
Every time I sang, vomit flew in
I turned the garbage bins upside down in my room
and had morning sickness, then had a smoke
My poetry books burned
Three hundred million babies were born
One hundred million of the young and the old died
The day I took the pills
I walked out the gate in the middle of my bath
Black plastic bags flew higher than a flock of sparrows
The discarded sewing machine was like the head of a horse
The sound of Mother's sewing machine
filled the holes in my body one by one
I tore off my swollen breasts and tossed them
beneath Mother's foot on the pedal
A forest gave off a foul smell, carried contagious diseases
It burned of fever during the night
A busboy at brightly lit Motel Rose
threw out millions of sperm every night
From the forest, mosquitoes swarmed
and dug into my scrawny caved-in chest
Born in the 20th century, I was on my way
to die in the 21st century

Daddy and Mommy lay us down one by one
Many of us are born—as many as Mommy's nipples
Mommy licks our eyes with her tongue softer than white bread,
licks with all her might, with darkness, darkness is cozy

Daddy who herds a fish head home also brings with him scary news
You can hear the footsteps far away, the wailing fire truck
Mommy's nipples harden
Mommy blocks the rat hole with her entire body,
our ears as well

A hairy leg enters our room It's him He thrashes his body around,
bam bam, shaking the house, but only the leg enters,
toenails rip Mommy's eyes, ears,
the foot in a leather shoe stomps on Mommy's skirt
Mommy isn't breathing

He pokes around, back and forth
as many times as the minute hand of the night
You can hear the snarl all night long
He wails, pounding his head against the wall
Mommy is like a corpse and Daddy is nowhere to be seen
All night long, crushed against the house,
a hairy mouth tries to get in

By morning all is quiet--he must have left
Mommy finally gets up and breathes
Mommy bites and kills each one of us
for giving off a suspicious scent from last night's terror
She kills us then eats our intestines,
grinds her teeth against a wall
then digs out our eyeballs to eat
then there is no one
As always, only Daddy and Mommy are left
It looks as if Mommy is expecting another litter

They're alive: — I'll talk about my invisible cats. They're alive. They lay two eggs every day. If they don't, they won't be able to multiply. After spring-cleaning, they're in danger of extinction. They disperse with a single puff. Yet, the cats are always alive in every corner.

They're very tiny: — I don't need to give them anything to eat. Because I who am visible always leave flakes of my dead skin for them. Because my cats are tiny enough to build an apartment inside a single clot of dead skin.

They barely survive: — They fall off when brushed off, they get eaten when sucked up, they put down their tails at the smallest cough. My cats are so tiny that when they are placed under a microscope and magnified 500, 1000 times you can barely see their adorable moving lips. There's one that is fairly big. It's floating in air but always at the fringes of the dust. It trembles, afraid it might get blown away when I let out my breath, even afraid to be touched by a feather. They are powerless against the cold. In summer, I can't even open the doors. They barely survive. Poor things. Please call me mother of cats. They're so tiny that I won't be able to embrace them. It can't be helped. I need to stow them in my pores at least. A red cat peeks out between the lines of a book. Such a cute thing. The cats are everywhere. They are in the center of my brain cells. Two eggs per day. Two eggs under a blanket. Red eyes, sweet cries. My cats that wiggle behind the sofa. When I return from school, they cover themselves with the dust blanket on top of the closet—the sound of them purring, crying.

However: — These adorable things. When my life gives out, they'd eat me up in a second. When it rains, they make me drag a leather sofa outdoors. They even build houses inside my nostrils. They'd even devour my elephant. They are like the stars that can't be seen in daylight.

At Mommy's house, the floors are also mommy, the dust that floats around the rooms is also mommy, when you open the door of Mommy's house I'm under Mommy's feathers like an unhatched egg. All the dreams that are dreamt in Mommy's house come from Mommy's fountain, the fountain at Mommy's house is never dry. Mommy weaves dream-nests so nicely with the feathers hauled from the fountain. Breakfast at Mommy's house: teacup is feathers, coffee is feathers, and even feather-teaspoons, feather-sandwiches, a winged breakfast.

Mommy who after teaching the children steps out onto the school grounds at dusk, carrying
   her empty lunch box
Mommy who on a Sunday breaks the morning ice and stoops down to flog and wash a
   blanket cover
Mommy whose hands are cracked
My spoon that floats around in the river that has melted
Mommy who has many other chicks, besides myself, dangling below her armpits
Mommy who lost her patience one night and went out to buy an electric incubator
Uncle who lives next door and checks the sex of the chicks killed all the males and sent them
   to a food stall where roasted sparrows are sold
All the female chicks were sent to a boarding house
He says the female chicks will be raised to be eaten later

Beneath sleep there are stars that have not hatched yet
Stars that call me desperately
Below the stars, far below
I, another mommy, have many cold stars in my embrace

When you open Mommy's kitchen door, there's a barley field
Green barley feathers are ripening
Every drawer is full of white fuzz from chicks just pulled out from the eggs
Fat feather snowflakes are falling under the wooden floor of the living room
A feather rainbow pours out from of the attic
I hang my nighties on the rainbow
My mommy weaves dream-nests really well
but I haven't been able to incubate my sleep
because my mommy keeps telling me to wake up quickly,
and says, "Let's eat a feather breakfast together, let's eat together"

Mommy who has just stepped out of the bath
A sleep that is soaked in drops of sweat like Mommy's skin
When I lay my head on my fluffy pillow on top of sleep
I am I before I was born
The sound of the red baby sucking her thumb
When the moon quietly rises and lifts my blanket
the windows rattle in sync with Mommy's breathing as she sleeps
The hem of the curtain trembles lightly
The moon enters the depth of my eyes
and strokes the fish flowing in every blood vessel
because it wants to touch the bones beneath my flesh
This must be the inside of Mommy's dream
The wave that rises and falls
The wave that is giving birth to a sea in the sea
The inside of Mommy's dream that gives birth to me like a rising tide
then embraces me like a receding tide then embraces me again like a rising tide
My body that will be swathed in the red fluid of the womb when the sun rises
When I lay my head down on my fluffy pillow on top of Mommy's
and Mommy's and Mommy's ripple

They came to eat the moon again
The women ate the moon and their bellies grew each month
They squeezed breast-milk into the moon,
  added the refreshing scent of mint to the roasted moon

I caught a glimpse of her kitchen once
The secretive chirp of the cooks dressed in white
The swirling storm severing the necks of wild ducks
on hundreds of wooden chopping boards
It was a sublime kitchen

A guest with a child entered
Mommy, mommy, can I have a glass of tangy star!
She brought out a drink made of powdered rain cloud
and floated an icy star in it

I caught a glimpse of her kitchen once
The rain cloud of flour mushroomed
and all kinds of dead animals' blood flowed down the drain
the cries of countless spoons, chopsticks, fingers, toes
got sucked into the dishpan
It was a sublime kitchen

It's time to prepare a midnight meal
She cracked the moon over the frying pan
a hole as deep as a fingernail appeared on the moon
then a flock of birds crawled out from the hole
with their wings that can be fried
The flock of birds spread their black wings
across the sky as the night deepened
She roasted the wings all night

Slobbered, chewed, licked, burped, chewed and chewed, sucked, tasted, drank, got fed
nonstop, swallowed and shouted Cheers! Eat more! Hey, Over here! One more bottle!
Smacked lips, belched, gagged

Like the lips that never once closed
the buildings on both sides of the street at night
the sound of them being fed the night sky through their huge openings
Everything was sublime

A rat
devours a sleeping white rabbit
Dark blood spills out of the rabbit cage
A rat devours a piglet that has fallen into a pot of porridge
(now, chunks of freshly grilled flesh inside a vagina,
babies that shiver from their first contact with air,
fattened chunks of flesh,
tasty, warm chunks that bleed when ripped into)
A rat devours the new baby in the cradle
Mommy has gone to the restaurant to wash dishes
A rat slips in and out of a freshly buried corpse

A rat that has never eaten anything that hasn't been stolen,
a rat that molds our shadows into a ball and blows into it to open our eyes,
a rat that silently burrows beneath the fungus in between the toes,
a rat that curls up its tail while eating voraciously even when it hears the rustle of a breath,
a rat that secretly watches us couple from behind a hidden camera,
a rat that has to grind its teeth daily, for they continue to grow,
that boasts it has seen entire eons of evolution

In between the tiny blood vessels inside our glaring exterior,
inside the dark slippery intestines beneath the soft skin,
in between the wiggling toes under the creaking floor,
inside the skull where the echoing footsteps of rain and wind hide out,
inside that dark place of my body that not even a single ray of light can penetrate,
inside that belly of the body of death tucked inside my body for years,
a rat grinds its teeth to devour the fingers

this night

As I raise my head, an old woman lying on the pavement is scraping off wads of gum

The glass window of a café divides us

I was walking along an unfamiliar street

then suddenly I went into the café to write a letter

A rat goes in and out of her body, raises a litter

The old woman is full of holes

Some days the rat peeks out from her lips

Startled, I jump up from the sofa

Mommy-rat has a baby-rat in her muzzle, climbing between the spring of the sofa

I tear off the rats and write a letter

The rats weave a delusion, a net that stretches endlessly the rats are playing you

Chase them away! I take a sip of beer the night arrives, but the old woman is still scraping off
    gum

I hear the rats are hiding beneath the ancient Buddhist temple

They wait for the day they'll be reincarnated as humans your death must have instructed
    them, for even death wants to live

Since you called them out, you should chase them away I keep writing my letter

The people getting off from work are swept away in waves, the people who will lose their
    sight when the light that is supposed to come comes

Perhaps roaming is endless only the lit windows are luminous like eyes that look into

themselves beneath the pavement, the rats' eyes gleam, looking into the night as if our night

is their home, and Jacqueline du Pré fills the café, trying to hold back her tears inside me the

rats must leave her stomach

As I raise my head, the old woman moves away she spits on the pavement, sneezing, and
    walks off, mumbling as if things are streaming out from her holes

Chase them away! Toss even the baby-rats!

Somewhere inside me, an empty bag bursts and a book flutters by I wonder what language it
    is in maybe the silent café of the goldfish has exploded

A stream of rats engulfs me

I begin to hiccup as if my lips are holding onto my heart

Enter the inside of the sunny morning, and it seems as if the scream can always be heard. It's so loud that it's inaudible to us. The scream let out by last night's darkness. This morning the whitish scream suddenly disperses then gathers in the air—*ah, ah, ah, ah!* Do people know how much it hurts the darkness when you turn on the light in the middle of the night? So I can't turn on the light even when the night arrives. The day of the first snowfall, I took an x-ray of my body. Then I asked everyone I met: Have you ever turned on the light inside your intestine? The darkness with a fluid mass moving through it endlessly—is this my essence? When the light is switched on inside my darkness, I buzz like a beetle pinned down, *bung, bung, bung, bung,* and shake my head wildly, my muzzle holding onto a black string. Struck by the light, I regress, in a flash, from a reptile to a beetle turned upside down. My dignity is the darkness inside. Was it hiding inside the darkness? Lights on—my underground prison, my beloved black being trembles in it. The damaged walls of my room quiver from the car lights coming in through the windows. Thousands of rays of light poke at me—my dark, crouched face. The day of the first snow, the snow was nowhere to be seen. The houses with lit windows. How painful the light must be for the night.

Rain hammers away at the keyboard till it's all bloody red mud splatters trees fall and the chickens tremble inside the water-filled coop she hammers away till the keyboard is bloodied she hammers away so hard that a crimson flower of flesh blooms on top of her skull the crown flutters like a flag, her heart placed on top of her head the lit window screams because the light in the room was turned off at one point her typewriter-teeth endlessly collect the feed onto the paper she lowers her head, feels her forehead three women left home today they left the coop crying you all know where they have been taken she spreads her ten fingers and clutches her desk, types the tears one at a time night arrives and the rain lets up her beloved's leather shoes drop outside the window and she lays an egg while hammering away at the keyboard the conveyer belt swiftly takes away her egg she mustn't go outside today her body, the book of pain, has barely made it through a page of flesh, bleeding, but the calendar she pecks out daily is still on the same page why is she making a calendar that no one looks at? her eyes want to sleep, so they close slowly from the bottom to the top outside the window, the rain, as if it had been lying in wait, begins to hammer away at the keyboard blood splatters on the window her eyes flash open and her heart, a loop of painful blood vessels, flinches and bleeds on top of her head the crown turns crimson once again

A poplar tree shakes its wet hair
in front of a mental hospital in Ch'ŏngnyangni
Maybe the night wind is blowing
the wind woven with the crazy birds' hair
I place a child in each lit window
and leave the hospital

the-crushed-chest-child the-lungs-filled-with-stones-child fluttering-like-a-ripped-ten-
fingered-fan-child the-lips-stuck-together-child the-eyeballs-melted-child the-teeth-
ground-down-child all-of-the-ribs-crushed-child all-of-the-hair-pulled-out-child especially-
all-of-the-blood-drained-into-the-sewer-child the-tongue-stretched-out-like-gum-child
all-of-the-brain-sucked-out-by-a-cat-child

The crazy birds put the crowns on each other
and circle in the night sky
A small child stood at the window of a small house in the forest
and a rabbit ran towards the house, knocked on the door, and said
I hear the songs of the children
Help us, help us
The song that pokes my throat like a continuous hiccup
In the middle of the mind of the crazy birds
my children who want to return to my body and lie down
the lit boat carrying the children floats silently

Again, I will call you my muse
The life span of each muse varies, but they are always alive
Muses multiply by themselves, they even produce litters
I call out the names of my muses one by one

Empty-match-box muse. Chocolate-wrap muse. Already-read-newspaper muse. Toshiba-laptop muse. 2-kg-laundry-capacity-washing-machine muse. Cooked-rice-container-called-Elephant muse. There is no end to crumpling the foil muse and calling it affectionate names. One muse was friendly enough to come up to me wearing a name tag, even a family genealogy paper. Nature-made muse, man-made muse, muse that Mother packed for me when I married. Still that is not enough, so I buy new muses daily. Sometimes, when it is too expensive, I pay by the month. It was tiresome waiting for the muse to be delivered. Anyhow, there are life spans to the muses. Many muses died next to me regardless of whether I gave them a name or not. My autobiography buys new muses daily, and it can only note that it has abandoned the muses that have died nearly every day. The big muses are filled endlessly with little muses. Do dead muses also produce litters?

My house in which a rice-cooker muse nurtures a maggot muse in my absence
A muse lays a muse, lays, lays again
Must take the forked lane in order to enter the house full of muses
My house that becomes a heaven of muses when the street sweeper doesn't come for ten days
My happy house in which my muses are left to fend for themselves—they glare at the
    opportunity to produce litters on the last day of the world

How about the collapsed-department-store muse? That place which became an embodiment of muses as soon as the walls crumbled. At least a statue of a muse-goddess should be erected. The conversations of people crushed under the muses inside the collapsed store. A woman whose thigh is caught between metal rods on the 3rd floor of the basement endlessly pages her pager and calls home on her cell phone: "Hello, hello, I don't think the phone is working…." I devote my life to washing, wiping, repairing, and ironing my muses. I discard the dead ones and take care of the live ones. I tidy them up, wash their faces, and hug them. I wonder if, someday, I might really become a muse myself, embraced by a muse. It is written on the back of the Chosŏn-Daily muse, which arrived in the morning, that the entire world has proclaimed the wars and corpses of the muses. The muses that will become wild when I die, the whole house full of muses that will fiercely multiply even after they are dead. Despite all that, this afternoon, I engraved the following on the back of a one-eyed-computer muse:

> When I moved, I abandoned
> a blue-eyed-black-cat muse
> because I heard that when a muse lives
> with you for a long time it turns into a ghost
> But after three days, my family saw
> the black-cat muse fly up to the window
> of our new house and cry all night long
> The eyes of the cat muse gleamed ice-blue
> intense enough to burn a hole through the glass
> Even the new-fridge muse shook
> with fear all night long

They are rummaging through the corpses. Those who ignite and hold the torchlights. Outside our sleep, the roads are wet from the rain, and they tear off our nametags. The torn-off nametags quickly pile up into a heap. Eyeglasses pile up with eyeglasses. Suitcases with suitcases. Shinbones with shinbones. Babies with babies who are thrown out into the future far, far away. The years that I've lived heap up, and on the side of the road a trial slowly goes on inside a green metal booth. A blazing bonfire. One of the janitors throws my book towards the fire. It flares up every time the book lands, and the leather shoes from which my feet have slipped, that used to roam around like a pair of fat married rats, give off a stench as they burn. The janitors who wear masks like the KKK, with a glowing cross on their backs, press down on my three meals with their feet. They sweep up the intestines that burst and spill out. My naked body folded tightly gets pressed down once again by their feet before heading for the gas chamber. The pressed corpses are placed in sacks then loaded onto a truck. Behind the door of my sleep, the Auschwitz of Seoul unfolds all night long. Teeth with teeth, fingernails with fingernails. The stench circles the same spot unable to disperse during the rainy night. The janitors finish up the job of sorting, load the corpses dripping with gravy, and take off down the road next to an apartment building. They need to hurry, for once again, today, the crematories are full and the grounds are already filled with corpses. The collapsed pink department store—we wept and clapped hysterically when the janitors like aged babies made it out alive from under the heap of 500 dead bodies. The saints, Mr. and Mrs. Janitor, who will live forever, tie me up—I who will utter "O Time"—and exit the sleeping city. The torn black sacks flutter like an elegy. Whose skull is this? A head with closed eyes falls from the truck and gets crushed again inside my dream.

Chickens die first inside the plastic greenhouse. Eggs rot on the conveyor belt. Rotten pigs packed in the refrigerated trucks are delivered to all the butcher shops, the dead float up in the aquarium. The farmer's market at Karakdong decays and the filth swells up inside my body and

you and I begin to rot in the open. I can't leave the lights on for you any longer. We can no longer look each other in the face. You are completely cut off from me. Our skin melts, so anyone can look into anyone's intestines. Toilets also overflow in dreams. Nothing goes down no matter how many times you flush. Even the candles give off a stench. If you have a flame thrower or a tidal wave,

please send it to me. Belgrade fell into darkness from the bombs that emitted black smoke. As the fighter jet dropped the bombs, the bombs exploded over the target and released black powder. The charged powder stuck to the power lines, caused a short circuit, burnt the lines, and disabled the power towers. NATO troops paralyzed the Yugoslavian troops' information network, scrambling their computer system. Inside a dim room where the computers sit not saying anything

crazy people increase in numbers. Birds shudder and fall off and flowers begin to eat worms. Furthermore, there are flowers that bite people. Here, below my feet, is the interior of the world. The dead chickens on the mud floor are strewn like mountains. Now, I throw salt at you—what little is left of you—inside my heart. Instead, the microbes that have remained dormant within my skin enlarge. They become as big as ants, then hedgehogs, and this morning they became as big as dogs.

The dogs bite off our remaining days and roam. Rotten nipples of the world's mothers drop like beans. Flies swarm what's left of the torn bodies. That is how pervasive darkness is. Ghosts eat food that has gone bad and stagger off as if being tied up and pulled away on someone's rope. Now you and I are merely shadows. Above the shadows, inside the sunlight, our silhouettes melt. We're alive, but our brains contain only lumps of rice that have gone sour. With all the forms destroyed, only the meanings bubble up from the honey bucket and fall, then bubble up again. Please send me a flame thrower or a tidal wave as soon as possible.

The house moves in. The house that can't be scooped out. The house across from us
is rushing in, reaching our family room. The whole family is trying to restrain the house, but it
has already swallowed up half of our house. The walls around the yard have disappeared and
the car is trapped in the house. Move the car! The man from the house across the street slaps
my face. The houses pile up like stairs and the stairs pile up inside the houses, the houses
endlessly flow in. The puppy that snuck outside was crushed to death by the houses moving
in. It has been a while since the alley where dogs can shit has disappeared. The corpses
that have just breathed their last are suffocated again by the houses rushing in and expire
once again. There is no empty land to lay down the coffins. There is no room for shadows in
my yard. Stand and hold up the walls. Daddy's arms are swollen from holding up the walls.
Mommy easily gets depressed and daddy beats mommy who sleeps all the time. However,
mommy is caught between the houses and can't run away, so she gives birth to her young.
Inside a room that is dark even though the window is hung in the air, my younger siblings
pucker their lips waiting for food like young swallows. My siblings who get hungrier as they
eat. On ancestor day, the ghosts can't breath, can't breath, so they can't eat either and return
to their underground apartments. From there the cries flow out daily, daddies make folksy
crafts that no one buys, and the sad music of the dead from the other world, the depths of the
underground, where corpses collect can be heard every night. Bricks pile up daily outside the
window and concrete pours into my mouth. The houses move in like the sand of the Sahara
that tumbles into an oasis. The houses that build houses inside my nostrils, earlobes, and hair.
When the wind blows, the overgrown roofs, the wavering pillars, the pulsating windows, the
antennas that transmit cries, and there is no one in Seoul—only neatly piled up houses.

In the middle of the night, a car speeds along a windy road. The people from the North who came over in a submarine—they've killed each other. This time a tunnel appears after the car goes down ninety-nine windy roads where the dead bodies are scattered. The car enters the tunnel. The end of the tunnel is not visible. The tunnel is dark. All the lights inside the tunnel are broken. I want to get out of the tunnel, the car shouts. The tunnel is round. The tunnel spins by itself. It's cold inside the tunnel. The car screams alone. An echo bounces back each time the tunnel spins around. Echo, echo. A swirling echo. It's damp in here. The car screams non-stop into the dampness. Even the car's headlights are turning. Dozens of them from the North had to kill themselves just because their submarine landed secretly in the South. Was the mountain this huge and heavy? It's as if the car had passed several underground mountain ranges. Right turn, left turn, right turn again. No one is following. Hold your breath. Curve, curve, cup…. there's nothing. At once the tunnel explodes black like a black aquarium. There is no mountain or tunnel. There is no road or sky. My entire body wants to shoot out of my face. I want to lie down. A scream floats up from somewhere inside my body. The car spins inside the tunnel within the body. Something leaps out from the inside of my body like the way a frog flattened in an illustration swells up into life. That thing, that slippery green light, that thing with thousands of heads, that thing with ten thousand fingers closes my eyes and ears and licks my face with its tongue. With its other tongue it licks my hair. It licks my chest. Its several hundred hands strangle me as it plants a heavy kiss on my eyelids. I let go of the steering wheel and clutch onto that thing. I bite into it. The car runs freely all by itself. If you look in from the outside, someone is fighting with an Asura. The Asura is not visible, but it's slippery. That invisible thing overpowers someone. Someone who is neither a man nor a woman grabs that thing and throws it out the window. That thing shatters into dirty green. The dirty green spreads to the east, west, south, and north. The car has left the tunnel, but there is no car on the road. Suddenly, it's spring!

We are always caught between June 25 and May 18
In between them music spins and goes insane as it spins
Inside my head, a prison riot
Electrical lines are clanging away
a searchlight flickers from the surveillance tower
That *vocal* is definitely out of his mind
Out of the blue
my students take me by the hand and pull me towards them, saying,
"Teacher, see how we are *banging* our heads"
Dust falls like the last days of Pompeii
it glitters then crumbles, it wavers then shatters and swirls
We face each other and release black balloons
we recite our names chanting, Let's not part from one another
The black balloons burst in air, leaflets fall out
Every time the vocal screams,
"I only exist inside your head
I'll get to see the hell within you for sure"
I say, "No, no"
Entire lifetimes flicker with a lamp in each hand
but all the days younger than today muss up my hair
Can't breathe unless I scream with all my might
It's our turn when the *vocal* falls silent
Inside that music,
the circle of June 25 and May 18 narrows as it repeats itself
that place where we'll vanish after we go round and round is the inside of my head
The prison heaves like a cat in a black garbage bag tied with the night's hair
A helicopter takes off and people in uniform circle the prison
We've missed the emergency exit

Where ever I meet you, you are always on the run
from Scorpio to Libra
from Libra to Taurus
Not here, not here
From the potato sack to the rice sack
from the soap dish to the bottom of the desk
from Lukács to Deleuze
from the basement to the attic
from the wastewater plant to the cemetery
I hate all things that are shiny and black
You are always on the run
from the deep to the surface

Where are you really?
Am I the dream you dreamt inside my body?
Am I the dream you pulled up with chopsticks from the 39 degree Celsius fever?
Did we meet as we gnawed on a corpse and rolled around inside the grave?
Where, where was that place?
Not here, not here
This is the inside of somebody's skull—
you can't look out without the two black holes

You say you will move from the age of Pisces to Aquarius
You pack every day, saying someday you will leave Seoul
Yet, tonight, in Seoul, where I am chased as if by a cat
we spill out from the Tongdaemun subway
get sucked up into somebody's flute

like a pack of rats

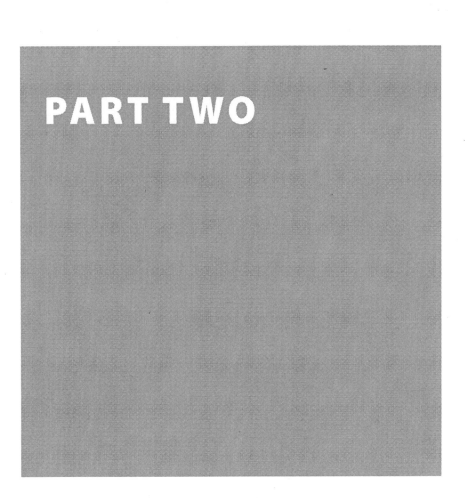

PART TWO

Child,
a hundred-year-old fox devours one hundred humans
and becomes a woman
I, a woman poet, devour one hundred fathers
and become a father
(How repulsive! Now I will have a five o'clock shadow)
I devour one hundred fathers,
and as I look around,
lifting high the knife of a narrative
sharpened by the teeth of fibs about the fathers
Look at you, entering between the sentences, riding a donkey
Eloi, Eloi!

Father returns from a field, where you are planted, after treating it with pesticide
Father chops off your arm and makes a wooden platform
Father chops off your lower trunk and sends it to a lumberyard
Father's hands are vicious blades
Father has acres to pace, wearing his big leather shoes
Father is startled when I say to him, "Father, play with me!"
I shout, "I don't want to become a father!"
But Father became a father because he'd killed father, his father's father
Steel-curtain-father, black-ink-father, machine-heart-father
Father has to bring his hands together sharpened like blades
in order to pierce my heart—that kind of father
Child, I've become such a repulsive Father

I came to find a peach in this life
I came to find the red stain, the stain from the bite
of the peach you spat out as you departed
They say you are sick in the world of ghosts
but I am in the frozen mountain valley of a snowy night
I think I must have been possessed by the field of snow
Where am I?
They say when you circle the entire field, red baby
becomes white grandma and white grandma becomes red baby
Peach blossom flurries, flurries of snow
fall and keeps falling again
and yet the endless white paper
The footprints of my life are erased as soon as they are made
The bloodshot eye opens somewhere deep in the ground
The hot thing that popped out from my womb
The pencil breaks, I have a lot of homework
But where is it really?
It seems as if the peach scent is coming from somewhere

#1   I press my nose and lips against the window, the third one down from the front, and watch the rain come down in the street.

#2   Fast flowing water says, "Pause it!" and stops.

#3   As the water splits in half

#4   catfish with headlights on in both eyes say, "Everyone stop! Line up in both directions!"

#5   Then goldfish carrying rainbow umbrellas cross.

#6   Air bubbles burst out bubble by bubble from the gills of red-finned tropical fish.

#7   They slide into a post office.

#8   I can't wipe the tears that flow down outside the window. I can't pass a handkerchief to you who lament on the screen.

#9   After a large #33 fish bowl passes by

#10   the waterway shuts down and the current picks up speed.

#11   Tiny fish, a newspaper peddler, its hair standing up like a rake, passes through an avenue of plastic trees.

#12   A fresh-water turtle drags one of its legs, for it suffered a stroke, and its left shoulder bends because of the slow video.

#13   Kissing fish line up in front of a phone booth, wagging their tails, and the line doesn't get any shorter.

#14   A strong current moves in and breaks the line to bits.

#15   The water level is rising, but I'm not scared because I don't get to hear your voice, only your silent hand-leg gestures.

#16   I press my lips against the rising water of the ever-changing television screen and look out at the street, the flooded street.

What happens if a white horse suddenly enters my room? what if the horse completely fills my entire room? what if the horse shoves me into its huge eyeball and keeps me in there? a shiny train enters the horse and dark people get off the train the sun fades and as the door of the deserted house opens she who is dark grabs onto her torn blouse and runs out and the stars amass around her ankles wait a second then she goes into the empty house and drinks pesticide then runs out and as she runs she tries to vomit out the horse by holding onto a tree but the horse never leaves once it has entered she's unable to cry she can only hiccup as the horse's mane may be tickling her throat what if the horse never leaves her body? what if the white horse grabs onto the paths engraved inside the body all night long and won't let a single train enter? what do I do? do I go and ask the woman who endures a horse inside her unable to say a single word because the pesticide has destroyed her vocal cords? here is my room but I can't enter or leave a horse aimlessly stands in the room

It's itchy somewhere far beneath the sea
As if the meal is being prepared for the umpteenth time
a fish is placed on a chopping board on the kitchen table
The knife comes down on the head—my skull is being severed
Instantaneously a blackout far beneath the sea
When the paths are extracted from the body on the chopping board
our rooms inside the sea that are like flowered wallpaper beneath a dim lamp
silently crumble
Blood faintly smears the chopping board
The crumbled rooms are a scandal
Put my finger into the mouth and pulled out its gills
I want to shove a finger into the silence and make it vomit
Now it's time to scrape off the scales with the blunt edge of the knife
Our paths inside the water that made our ears itch crumble into bits
I runs towards me inside of my body again
and is banging against the door
It seems as if the heart has become a junkyard
It seems as if the inside of the body is aging at high speed
I mishandled the knife—the scales splatter on the kitchen floor
I took out the intestines. Shall I take off the skin?
I didn't think deeply about it at all, but I ended up slicing the flesh
What do I do? The fish has shattered

White snow. White rabbit. White night because white snow fell overnight. White rabbit stares at white steel-barred window. White gown. White sheet. White wrist. White hat. White skirt. White legs turning. White sandal. Gave birth to a white baby because of white snow. White rice that you eat while holding a white umbrella. I ate it--a white pill that makes white blood. White God inside white snow rises as high as the window. There is a white secret inside white snow. White blanket. White sweat. White skin of baby Jesus. The white wall is too high. White lips. White nose. There are too many white rats in white milk. White breath, can't breathe. There is no road because white snow keeps coming down. White devil. White hell. It's too far. White yawn. White sleep. Please untie white bandages. White writing on white paper. I will erase my white poem. Oblivious innocence of White God, open my blood's path outwards.

It's remarkable
Every morning I open my white eyelids,
squeeze out white toothpaste,
and shove it against my white teeth as I
tear open a white tent and walk out the door

White shovel inside white snow. One white house. White window. White lamp inside a white curtain. White grandfather, please eat. White bread sent from God. White butterfly. Butterfly. Butterfly. Butterfly. Mother, please look at the white butterfly. My god, how can this be? How many days has it been? White mother. White cough. White sigh. White breasts. White powdery snow slides in back of white ears and falls softly softly on top of a desk. White snow is falling. Young white woman's white smile. White birds land and pile up one by one. Closed eyes of the birds. White bird is pressing me down. It's too heavy. Please remove the blanket. Jellyfish multiply inside the sea. Sea becomes firm like jelly. White sea. Sea crumbles like white powder. White rabbit on top of white sand. White wrist. White needle.

White snow fills up
the white snow wall fills up
but I keep pushing the white wall high high up into the air
Where is the end of my old civilization?
Hell of tenderness
A white ant that fell into white sugar hell
White sugar melts
White sugar hell binds the white ant like honey
Can't breathe

"I like A," I said.

Then B ran towards me and hit me.

When I said, "B hit me because I said I liked A," C ran towards me and beat me.

When I said, "B hit me because I said I liked A, and because I said B hit me C hit me," A ran towards me and beat me.

When I said "B hit me because I said I liked A; because I said B hit me C hit me; and A hit me because I said C hit me," A, B, C, all ran toward me and beat me.

Now I had no choice but to get beaten up and pant, "They got me, they got me."

And I couldn't even remember who it was that I liked.

Even though there is no wind the leaf of a weeping willow shakes. Two leaves of a weeping willow shake. Three leaves of a weeping willow shake. Four leaves of a weeping willow shake. Even though there is no wind the entire weeping willow shakes wildly. Weeping willows crowd the empty riverside, shaking wildly.

He arrives from the distant Mongolian plains. The sound of his horse's hooves gently sways the ends of my hair. I pray with my eyes open. Please forgive my heart. I watch the trembling weeping willow while praying. From morning till afternoon I stare at the weeping willow.

The leaves are like flying fish. They glisten. Everything glistens. A lightening bolt passes through the trunk of the weeping willow. Perhaps someone is trying to weld the leaves. Green flame explodes in all directions then crumbles as if a furnace boiling with green light has been toppled.

I mumble louder and louder, Please make it stop. A leaf of the green beam must have stuck to my eyes. My eyes are open, yet I'm blind. The sound of hooves becomes louder and louder. He is crossing the river. I pray with all might till my heart whistles. Now I pray shouting, Please make it stop.

The weeping willows jump up and down. Beneath my feet is a deep-blue river. I am at the top of a cliff, mumbling. Green sap pours from my eyes. The sound of the whip against the horse's sides. Green scales splatter everywhere. I stare at the weeping willows across the river till night, mumbling.

At the riverside a woman is taking off her green socks. The socks are so long that no matter how hard she tries to take them off they can't be removed. The woman's hair is the leaves, the leaves are on fire. Suddenly she turns her head, even the sun turns around. Then the woman quickly swallows me with her long tongue. While I am dizzy inside the darkness of the green, an egg made of light spins around in my eyes. Where am I? I am riding a green horse at the bottom of the river.

leave Buddha alone? We make Buddha ride an elephant like the way a village boy rides on a man's shoulder, and we let the Buddha run and play, then make him cry, and we make him couple blissfully with a buttery woman and call it Tantra, but then we make him smile by himself in emptiness, make him sit, lie down, make him be born from the waist, then teach him how to walk right away, and we question him when he lies down to sleep You said this and that didn't you? and we braid his fingers, cut off his nose and swallow it down with water, then dress him in gold, but then we cut his throat and sell his head at a store in Insadong, and we lock him up inside a cave on top of a mountain, and as if that weren't enough we keep him inside a rock, starve him, paint his skin gold so that he can't even breathe, have him stand faraway on top of a mountain and caress him slowly as we approach him by boat, and beneath his feet we beg him to beat us up. Why can't we leave him alone? We build a house on a cliff overlooking a blue river and lock him up and a bunch of us go together to gawk at him. We pummel him, crush him, and push him over, then we come home and write a letter of apology in blood from our pierced fingers, and we pull his teeth and divide them up into numerous pouches and give them out to the whole world, and why do we go near him and bow on our knees till they are raw and look once into his eyes then return home with our downcast faces?

Run, holding, only, your, lit, ten, ta, cle, blue, and, cold. Go, run. Give, your, bodies, to, mag, gots, that, feed, on, bodies, sell, frenzied, your, legs, to, people, who, come, to, buy, legs, and, shout your bids. Vomit, excrete, dribble, give, away, everything, every thing. Pull out and show, your, wick. Run. Sick, Body, when, someone, calls, you, shout back, I'm alivealive. Don't, arrive, just, de, part. Run, so, that, the, needles, can, slip out, white, beds, can, crumble, bloody shit, can, splatter, and, dead things, and, stench, can, fly, high up, in, the, sky. Life, leavesthenreturns, departsthenarrives, and, the, sick, body, burns, up, then, takes, on, life, and, runs, out, again! Look, over there, there. Happiness, painted, in oil, is, inside, a frame, and, now, sa. ccha. rine. Of happiness, flows, like. a. ri. ver. Into, my, blood. If someone, asks, Is anyone alive? Break, your, head, open, and, show, your, ten, ta, cle.

Sick

      bodies

          that

             keep

                talking

                    in

                        their

                            sleep

                              !

God raised cows on a ranch in the sea
The cows fattened leisurely eating grass
There were no herders, no fences
We couldn't see even with our eyes open
but every cow's head was branded with God's seal
God played a flute when night came
All the blue cows were gathered
God scoffed at all the cows

I stole one of the cows and
gave it to a Mongolian who
with one hand kept the lamb's mouth shut
and with another made a hole in its heart
He said, this cow belongs to the sea
It has no fur, no flesh. We don't eat anything from the sea
The cow belongs to him—his body made entirely of tears
The lamb he caught was skinned
without a single drop of blood or a scream

This time I had no choice but
to eat the blue cow by myself
My body became covered in blue mold
I couldn't feel the cold and roamed the streets in sub-zero weather
Except for the salt crystals falling from one of my eyes
The sea grabbed my ears every where I went
and rippled all day
I couldn't sleep at all

The crushed body gets erased
then is crushed again
like the way a painter holds and shakes a thin brush
and keeps drawing thin lines
in order to keep lifting up
the body about to be crushed

Inside Café Pulp, the chairs are as narrow as bathtubs
That person looks like he's imitating a fish
His lips pucker, blowing out rings of cigarette smoke
That person is like a dog soaked in rain
barking alone, grabbing the phone attached to the tub
The phone is silent like a red aborted infant
I want to hide the phone under my skirt

I start a conversation with someone who
I would like to have in front of me
"Please think again"
I lick that someone's wet hair
with my tongue which is like a dirty mop

The searchlight strokes our hair once
and I hold up my arms
like a sleepwalker
head towards the metal fence
made of water
Those poor love machines
are still barking
like chained dogs

Naturally, rain fell from the sky
(However, she didn't get wet)
She took a bus to her house
(She didn't have a home)
All the passengers on the bus had a home
(However she didn't have a home)
The windows of the bus are segmented like a cartoon
(The cliffs with numbers attached to them honked and sped up)
The bus soon arrived at the terminal
(However, in truth the bus didn't have a terminal)
She stopped in front of her house
(Her house shook as though it were hanging from a swing)
She quietly rolled up her face then tucked it between her legs
(She didn't have legs)
Was her house hiding inside her body?
(The house grabbed her by the throat)
Everywhere I step is my home—did she believe this?
(There was no floor to spread a blanket out on in her house)
Was the road a home for her?
(She just stood there holding her house)
Ripples continuously spread above the roof
(Her house didn't have a roof)
Her house flowed down from the crown of her head like blood
(Who pulled out the house?)
Doors fell
(However, in truth her house didn't have any doors)
The doors flowed downstream
(The river was crammed with her doors)
Her house that quietly crumbles into the river
(Where have you been your whole life?)
A lifetime of rain from the sky

(However she didn't get wet)
Her house that she can't even live in
(Her house that is draped with her eyes)

You come every night to use this machine
a machine without a door
yet like a ball
you can jump into it
but as soon as you enter, you get to eat death
The machine eats you, eats
Do you know that you don't exist?
You have fallen asleep in an oasis
but when you wake up it's always a desert

When you place your hand on the machine it comes alive
The whole machine lights up
like the nightscape of New York from Empire State Building
You move about fiercely inside me
like an ambulance with lights on
like Halley's Comet swimming between the stars
The throbbing city, the shivering valley of stars
The inside of my body glistens

However, don't be deceived
You should at least have a cold beer first
Have you ever opened the drawer of this machine?
Inside it there are thousands of metal balls
that look like you
All of them belong to the poor love machine

Do you feel as if you control
the planets that tremble faintly in the night sky
Do you feel as if you're betting on the whole of life?
Don't be fooled, don't fuss
for the machine is merely following
its self-preservation program
There is no place inside the machine just for you
The only thing for you to do is to keep returning to the beginning
swimming through the eternally empty body made by the machine
without a door

Flowers enter. The flowers with puckered lips. The flowers that fill the back of a truck suck on the wall of the tunnel. The tunnel reddens momentarily. She plucks off the new leaves and shoves them into her mouth. Angelica shoots drop from angelica trees and fall into the dish of seasoned soy sauce. A truckload of angelica enters. Angelica shoots turn the mouth of Seoul green. Flatfish enter. A thousand flatfish packed in ice enter, swooning. A truckload of the East Sea enters. Pigs enter. The pigs oink and suck on Seoul's lips. She dips the meat from the pig's neck in pickled shrimp and eats. Her squirming throat is omnivorous. Mudfish pour in like a muddy stream. The Taebaek range is shredded and enters, squirming. The fields of the higher ranges of Mount Sŏrak enter, salted. Radishes revealing only the top half of their white bottoms are neatly stacked onto a truck. Trucks with their lights on enter. They line up and enter in between the teeth. When the trucks leave the tunnel, Seoul's blue stomach acid embraces them. Some of the trucks with big eyes try to make their way through the sea of acid, but the darkness inside Seoul's intestine is dense. Greens in sacks enter. Thousands of chickens with reddened crowns follow thousands of eggs just laid today and enter. Bulls as big as elephants their eyes fiercely opened enter. Bulls charge the path inside the body of someone who lives in Seoul. Tonight she drinks too much soju. The tunnel where the liquor is poured is long and dark. White milk that could overflow Lake Soyang pours out of the tunnel into the night's intestine. The plains of Honam enter. But in the opposite lane, trucks loaded with waste water purifiers have lined up in single file. Having left the party, I begin to vomit as soon as I step outside. Seoul eats and shits through the same door. My body curls up like a worm. It seems that every few days a big hand descends from the sky to roll out cloud-like toilet paper and wipe the opening of Seoul, which is simultaneously a mouth and an anus. Tonight, fat flakes fall as the last truck leaves the tunnel. I let the snow collect, then shove it into my mouth.

A black fishnet stocking moves to four in the afternoon. Skip, skip, as if someone is endlessly counting, the stocking moves to four o'clock. It has to go down the stairs and keep bending both legs. Four o'clock has not yet arrived. But the black fishnet stocking politely waits its turn in front of a black piano.

The black fishnet stocking moves to seven in the evening. Seven o'clock waits for the stocking with its legs folded. The black stocking begins to sing. Inside the restaurant, the world of the black stocking is spacious. The open land breathes like a hill wet by rain and the districts with tiny breathing holes are packed with houses. More customers appear and seven o'clock squirms. As the stocking grabs the mike, many more lit houses appear in the fishnet districts and a poor baby honeybee falls asleep in one of them. In front of that house, cars speed by along the eight-lane highway. As the night deepens, no one listens to the stocking's song. As the black stocking shakes the swollen legs beneath the mini skirt, a drunk customer lifts one of his fingers and rips the stocking.

The black fishnet stocking moves to eleven o'clock. As a rule when the night arrives, the film projector is pointed towards the inside of the body. The black stocking that receives the light from the projector inflates then deflates. The black stocking blows out cigarette smoke. Inside the smoke, all the houses with lights off on top of the hill appear. But the cry of the baby honeybee rises from the depths of the darkness. Every time the cry is let out, the holes woven with black string expand infinitely then shrink into a small clump. The song that no one listens to echoes throughout the night. The black stocking that is still breathing rolls up like crumpled paper and gets trampled under the feet of the drunk customers.

I look into the fish tank where I used to live. A tank that returned to me with its arms folded when I stretched out mine. How did I end up standing outside the tank that day? I looked at the tank, a mirror that is alive. A tank that pressed down on my body for a lifetime. In 1999, water flowed out from my body. Almost as if my body were someone who had pulled out a body from a swimming pool. My body melted down outside my clothes. I buried the tank between my knees and cried. The tank became more slippery. It looked like someone else's face. Then your face slipped out from my tank and your eyes evaporated, and, in my hands, your skull crumbled into powder and melted away like dough. I watched the skull on my knees cry like a cracked fish tank. A few years after 2029, didn't my heart burn up like a desert at midday? When I awoke in the morning, you opened the window of my heart and threw in hot sand. Didn't dried babies' breath fall out when I opened my mouth? Then several years later, maybe it was 2048, I carried the tank, and, as I crossed a frozen sea, didn't a stallion made of ice stand up beneath the frozen sea as snow turned to hail inside the blood vessels? Then several decades later something that made the white table cloth black, something that smelled rotten gazed into the fish tank.

When I'm about to doze off, I hear footsteps coming up the stairs inside my body, houses that get startled even before the lights are off, shoes that can be seen in the dim light, doors with their eyes half closed Pacman is coming up the stairs he walks up, eating
up the dotted lines inside a maze he comes up the inside of a video-drome made of flesh a horizon of sleep extends below the houses of my life drown below the horizon inside the maze of two gloomy brains, the flies that have devoured me at last and that are about to shoot up from the ground remain submerged and even the sun that has risen up the stairs of the sky for millions of years remain submerged in water Pacman the outlaw jumps up above the horizon of sleep Pacman, find the exit this game will end if you find the exit Pacman goes back into the water he stops and flings open a door I, a naked child, shiver shiver a train whistles and enters a railway station there Pacman kicks a barricade that keeps me hidden Pacman breaks through and attacks every time he changes his direction my body's rooms get turned on and off like lit-up squares a room bright with fall colors closes and a room of snowstorms opens a tear-filled spring begins to shine a bellybutton turns on the light I lie down and turn, hugging my chest with my two hands maybe because Pacman's black knife has struck my chest a blanket falls down to my feet and the horizon of sleep shoots up above my body time plays me like a VCR with the Pacman locked in I open the curtain locked inside the lit square, I look out at Seoul which is still dark

A hole walked in just as I was wiping off my makeup
I looked at the hole as I sat on the sofa and took off my stockings
The hole was about one meter and sixty centimeters wide
I hear the hole makes good steamed rice
and on some days babies pop out from it
However the hole isn't certain whether someone is spitting into it or not
and even when a black cloud sits leaning against its thighs for decades
it doesn't care
A fool, like a hell that keeps on walking
I poured left-over seaweed soup into the hole
Really the hole is nothing an idiot but it's deep
When I took out my wisdom tooth a one-meter-and-sixty-centimeters-wide hole
opened up
However the problem is that a hole falls into the hole endlessly whenever it can
Where's the hole's end?
The hole remains a hole even if the water from all the ponds of the world is poured into it
Do people know that the hole puts on makeup?
That it cries when it is hit by lightening?
That a red tongue that detests the hole hides inside the hole's mouth and kneads an ohohoh
    sound?
The hole intensifies when it stays in bed too long
In other words the hole becomes deeper and deeper
When I get up in the morning I see a mark on my pillow
from the tears of the hole

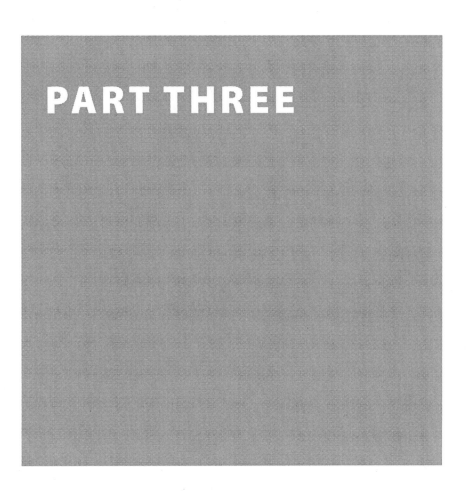

PART THREE

The main ingredient of my social standing is reaction
Night after night I go to school to write the confession of my crime
My lover, a photon, is a Red Guard who enjoys digging
The photon has many lovers, dispatched from the sun
to the inside of my dream, maybe it's a prison guard or a murderer
After copulation, it devours its lovers
Even though I confess my crimes day by day, there are always more left

I'm so exhausted today. My eyelids feel like a ton of bricks and my ears pull down the shutters, the photon that has been pacing outside my dream knocks on the door. Photon, please, I'm worn out today. After a long day of roaming inside sunlight and being crushed by the photon as flat as a screen, the photon inserts a confessional program into my body. I'm too sick today, just forgive me, please. The photon makes a hole in my body, goes deep into my flesh with a spade and bangs on my bones with its beak. The photon that is as bright as a star. The photon that flickers on the TV screen after the broadcast has ended. The photon calls my name, gets furious at me, encircles me, blabs to its heart's content. The confession that I write again and again. The photon enjoys itself, uses the waterfall of my blood for its mirror. I've written so many confessions that I don't know what's what. Things are mixed up to the point that my father is transformed into my child. How wonderful it would be to sleep even one night outside the house of the photon. A few decades ago, when I used to work for a publisher, I went to the city hall to get the manuscripts inspected. Mr. Military Officers with black ink would hand me back the pages after smearing ink all over them. Sometimes the entire manuscript was blackened except for the title. Where did all the blackened Mr. Officers go?

The photon plays all night, using the inside
of my body as a screen, and today it has made
my dead grandmother much younger than me
Grandmother took out a charcoal briquette from the furnace
then replaced it with the full moon on fire
Inside the room, Mother lay down after giving birth and cried
There were people inside each teardrop, so I asked,
"Who are you?" They replied that they were Mother's spirits
But when I looked closely into the teardrops, the people were all me
Inside the closed school, I was sitting on all the benches
reading aloud from my confessions, and the voice informed me that
Grandmother grows up and becomes Mother
and Mother grows and becomes me
There are so many of me that I feel like I'm going to die
Every night I collectively
go to school to write confessions
go to the photon to get censored

I missed my stop from thinking of you
Rain fell as I pressed the bell stop, Please let me off
People in the street walked slantwise
Their screams as I jumped into the rain
The birds that talk inside the throats of the people running peeked out
Each of them shouted, I don't want to live inside someone else
A man followed a woman and a woman followed a woman and
a woman ran, following the previous man
Mr. who got off the same bus behind me followed, calling me, Sis, Sis
The handkerchief in front of his chest flapped like a flower with a broken stem
The sky with a damaged immune system coughed away
Dark spots below the thighs were spreading
All the clock hands attached to the rooftops slanted to the right
A previously frozen lump of clay began to melt
Ugly faces fell and splashed down onto the ground and rolled about
The birds that live inside other people's bodies flew up all together
They spat as they kept shouting
My head that used to think about you spreads to the rest of the street

There is another you inside you

The you inside you pulls you tight into the inside, so your fingernails curl inward and your outer ears swirl into the inside of your body you would probably leave this life the moment the you inside you lets go of the hand that grabs you

Your face stays frozen in motion as the you inside you pulls you hard at times, that face leans towards mine outside of you and I can feel the you inside you looking at me from the inside of your eyes; but the you inside you has never once let go of the hand that grabs you as always you are pulled tight now your face has deep creases from the strain

The you inside you is so strong that the I inside me is about to get dragged into your inside

Now you are drinking a glass of red wine, holding a piece of cheese in your hand

The I inside me thinks about the fact that the cheese is made of milk then worries about which cow inside the cow has spurted out the milk

Even if you are far away, another you inside you is here I can't return or avoid the you inside you

Maybe I am the hostage of an absent being

I will certainly stay alive while the I inside me clutches onto me; furthermore, I want to deliver the cheese made of me inside me to your table every morning

Someone is taking out
a question from a question mark.
Question that flew like a chicken feather,
question that gave its body to the wind,
question that stripped naked,
question that painted the entire body,
question with a hidden face,
question that cried.

Question's tears. Tears' flood. Question's knee. Pull up the knee, question. Turn over, question. Good, question. Bark like a dog, question. Question, open your mouth. Question's saliva. Saliva's flood. Question, careful with the knee. Question that bites off a question. Don't sleep, question. Sing, question. Flap around like the wind, question. Comma, enter here. Block the question. Don't let it out, comma. Question, question, back in place. Singing question. Question that left a period. Question that is lonely from one remaining question. Question made up of a tail. Question with a tail up after the rain. Oh poor question that bit its lip while being blown about.

A period that lost a tail
cries silently.
Now someone draws near a period
and tries to shove in
a fallen question.

On that day white paper got stamped as always *ppang ppang* and that day wine glasses also were filled then emptied and the women pulled down their skirts and shouted Get your hands off of me and that day as always he rolled down the car window and spat and the chair spun and multicolored ties flapped like flags and the 9 o'clock news showed 59 men's white shirts and shoeshine boys spat on shoes to shine them

She is pregnant with the enemy soldier's baby she only takes naps her belly keeps growing her breasts get bigger because no one has given her the stamp she is not permitted to do anything so she can't go to the supermarket to the movies to neighborhood association meetings she got her head shaved she got dragged around the streets she endured each day that no one came home her eyes became big like a water buffalo's because she's in her last month of pregnancy she goes up to the 25th floor as her baby begins to come out

A water buffalo jumps from the roof of the 25th floor the camera of the Animal World follows the buffalo that is chased by a lion the buffalo giving birth to its young ends up being chased by a pack of lions the calf that poked out its head and front legs from its mother died from shock so the buffalo without hands unable to pull the rest of the dead calf from its womb roams the field with the front-half of the calf still hanging from it Please pull out my dead calf the buffalo collapsed then moved about and collapsed again the field of hot sun quickly decomposes the dead calf the herd of buffalos has crossed the river long ago alone mommy buffalo's eyes become bigger and bigger

The ambulance is loud
The fire truck is even louder
The buildings shoot up daily like canes
They say men cut those canes
to whip the women
The long scream of the asphalt road in the middle of the night!
Go straight and it's Namsan Tunnel Number 3
Turn right and it's Tunnel Number 2 or Sowŏl's Way
I asked in front of the road sign
So where am I?
Like my mommy inside my dim memory
the subway station is brightly lit with its heart open
At night the rain clouds have that look
like they have so much to endure
From the dark underpass
someone's cold breath rises up all night
like the sea cave that has lived for thousands of years
only listening to the waves' demands
or perhaps like the ear that can only hear imaginary voices
The Han River at night is perfectly yellowish
like the belly of a woman who has been whipped
I am night, roaming
the streets of Seoul naked
The wind that gets delivered somewhere as life or death
is louder than a motorcycle gang
The screen that displays today's casualties
from automobile accidents suddenly updates the figures
and they say the guardian angel of Seoul who lives hidden
somewhere licked his chops over a few victims
If I fill up at the gas station that looks like a beetle on fire
will I be able to take off to the top of the pulsating roofs?

The ambulance must not sleep at all—it's really loud
But wait, would you please insert this line into the scenery?

I cry out to you from a deep place

I'm desperately holding back the urge—my feet want to reach you before me. I'm desperately holding back the urge—my lips want to reach you before me. I've held back like this for decades. It's strange when I think about it. It seems that I've been holding back since I got a fridge of my own. Anyhow, I've been thinking. My head is completely filled with ice. Anyone who touches my cold feet faints. The lips of those who enter my heart freeze. Therefore, I won't budge from here. I won't hold out my arms to anyone. I think to myself that I won't forget any of this. Because I'm desperately holding back like this not a single leaf drops in my room, not a single bird can take off from the ground. I'll hold out with my fingers plugged into the 220-volt outlet even if the wind blows. The frozen painting of a landscape, how beautiful! The ice princess of the ice world inside the landscape, how pure! I won't worry even if blood drips down her thighs because it will freeze right away. It's hot outside and cold inside. It's so cold that it's boiling. When the door opens, I'm so startled that I turn on the light, frozen intestines hang from the winter landscape. The power has been out for several days because of the typhoon, and for decades I've been acting as if nothing's wrong till the inside of my body begins rotting away.

You fly deep into the night sky
I can detect your heat while I sleep
A cruise missile has launched!
The heat of explosion far above the sky!
Soon the water in a pot boils
I can't sleep, so I might as well have a cup of coffee
I almost dip my hand into the boiling water
for the boiling water looks so cold
Instead I dip my head inside the pot and say something
Are thousands of layers of ear membranes boiling?
Or are they a metaphor for birth and death?
Thousands of Morse codes undulate in the evaporating boiling water
It is like the Mass in a cathedral
The condor shoots straight up against the harsh air streams
slowly circles, then rapidly descends
and looks down distantly at the boiling water
Maybe someone has hidden a helicopter in the forest
From faraway the sound of the trees boiling
The thousands of electrical wires are pinned to the body's interior
begin to emit electricity to the inside, inside
this is not just a feeling but an ultrasound, a hydro-current
my inside can get electrocuted when I place my hand in it
this time I begin to boil like an electric pot
this isn't love but an electricity detector, a missile
Hear a boiling sound from the ear
Swish, swish, I escape from my body
All the water evaporates

Where does life hide inside me?
Where does life hide inside the black garbage bag
tied with hair as black as night?
The janitors empty the bag in the middle of the street
and pick through the garbage
as if they are trying to catch the murderer
who has secretly thrown away a corpse
Actually things that have been thrown away tell us plenty
They say people who live on mutton on the prairie
can even predict tomorrow's weather when they cut open the sheep's belly
and look at its gut
I took a train, I ran away into the nightmare landscape
sealed inside the garbage bag
The trees that are as sharp as cut fingernails
the feminine napkins that have wiped the blood-red waves
the wingless birds of night that have descended like
white Kleenex that fall out of a square blue box
the film that is rolled up like an endless track
the movie that is screened somewhere inside me
where does life hide?
Inside the garbage bag I was struggling
to be reborn though I wasn't even born yet
When the caterpillars of winged insects fell out of the bag
the frightened janitors stepped back
and the smell of the dream that never rots
colored the night street
where does life hide inside me?
The black garbage bag seized by thousands of hairs
stands alone in the street

A landscape strolls on me
I stroke the night landscape
On a rainy night, the landscape turns around in bed
Why is the landscape here and not there?
The landscape breaks out in goose bumps
It continues to tremble even when I hold it in my arms
Why does it want to enter my body and start suffering?
The landscape dangles the subway from its waist, the rain pours in
Outside the subway
A night landscape of
rusted metal skulls with messy hair, dripping red water from their stale nipples
and below, a bleeding broken bottle that has wiped its mouth
I am standing there, inside the landscape, without an umbrella
As I bury my face in my pillow
the distant, invisible Mount Kwanak steps aside and another landscape appears
It looks as if there is depth to the landscape
It gets deeper daily, digs into the pit of the stomach
The landscape changes with every breath
Fog blooms and my room melts and flows down the river
Why does suffering become such a junkyard
when it leaves my body?
The inside of the landscape that spouts out from the inside
I don't know why I find myself leaning against the unfinished concrete wall of Ujŏng Hospital
    that is spitting rusty water while rain slaps my face
The sensitive skin of the landscape that changes when I stir
Yes, now I'll lock the door of the landscape
I was happy when I watched you from afar
but when I got closer
the landscape of night rain in my arms
cried without me, panted without me
There, in the middle of the landscape of night rain

with all the blood of my body heaving in and out
I walked by and cried loudly like a deaf woman
Several rain clouds flow down my face
A landscape that has only one side
But then where is the exit?

1.

Q: It's inside an eye, isn't it?

A: That's right. That's why my soul lives looking only at my irises.

Q: The soul may also be inside a heart.

A: Of course, my soul lives only to gaze upon my heart.

Q: Who do you think you are—Confucius, Mencius? You think you can dispute every point? The soul may be attached to the end of a penis.

A: Of course. You're absolutely right. I shot my own soul for the sake of my child. I have no soul.

Q: (As if dreaming…) The soul may have dissolved into my bodily fluids. When you curl up like a fetus and cry, I see a bit of your soul flowing out with the tears.

A: Yes, it must have turned to water. Yesterday when I spilled my soul on a dining room table, you wiped it off at once with a dishcloth.

Q: Some say that when a person dies, the soul becomes a bird and flies away.

A: I've never heard before that the soul is an egg-laying mammal.

Q: This is something I've just thought of. The soul must have permeated my entire being. We are like caterpillars. After we die, we become butterflies and fly away. We'll flutter away like this! You, a white butterfly, and I, a tiger butterfly.

A: Oh, I never knew God had such an interest in collecting butterflies like me. After I die, I'm going to become a spider. I'm particularly interested in tasting tiger butterflies.

2.

I pour seaweed soup over cold rice,
stir it around with a spoon and chew with my mouth open,
and search everywhere to catch your soul.
Sometimes as I search I lose my way inside the soup
and shove in my head.
The soul nearly gets caught in the spoon,
but shrewdly seeps into the heavy rice,
floats light on the air, no,
heavily beneath the stomach.

3.

caterpillarandcaterpillararemakingcaterpillarlovebutifcaterpillarbecomesbutterfly willitlovelikecaterpillarlshedcaterpillarandflyhighupmadlywillbutterflyrecognize caterpillariscaterpillarskinevenyouaresheddingcaterpillarandflyingoverhereis caterpillarmotherorsonhowwilltwocaterpillarsandtwobutterfliesresolvetheirlove

It was already too late when I dug into the grave, the corpse that had already been devoured by rats showed up and my back ached. The organs inside the back ached, the organs shrieked and rattled the bones, and a hired man said that, if I wanted to find a fat rat, I needed to turn this cemetery inside out. It was fashionable to have babies in your forties and, strangely, azaleas blossomed from a rose bush and acacias smelled like lilacs. Pyökje Cremation was in great demand and mismatched legs kept arriving and piling into the coffin and in one coffin there was only the hand of a woman. The beautician was dead on her feet. I flew to Spain to watch flamenco and watched it again as I rotated once, for 12 beats, rotated twice, for 24, and repeated, "O Time, be gone, be gone," and from where I was sitting I wished for many lifetimes to pass. My lover would only talk to me in code and a Japanese critic was up in arms, "That's just how I am. What's your story?" Even though I was told that scorpions were submerged inside the rain-soaked mud, I rooted in it and smeared it on my face. The president of each country signed an exchange so that the corpses of dead husbands could be returned as Christmas gifts from the war-torn country and my students shouted towards the screen "Nature!" But my fellow poets ripped the screen and shouted towards the darkness, "Here is nature," and we carefully considered whether the remaining enemy of Father was also our enemy. While we were deep in thought, only the women factory workers who weren't hooked up to the internet bought fiction. Then one day, I raise the lid of the manhole that empties into the canal. The rats that open their eyes only in the dark, their eyes that have turned the color of sewage, their teeth that have become sharp as picks from digging around with their black eyes open. The rats startled by the light trickling in run away with their hairless litters that have just opened their eyes in their mother's embrace and

I wonder if such thing as depth can be measured in this universe
I hear this planet falls daily into space at full speed
Sad rain fell all day
and toilets overflowed in my dream
It was desolate and nothing froze even though it was winter
The KBS Sunday Special showed North Korean children who snatched up noodles
from the muddy ground
This is a scene after the nuclear explosion,
my daughter shouted towards the TV screen, slowly shaking her head like an old woman
This time I was watching a film called Freeze, Die, Come to Life
The people in the film sang badly written songs day and night
Mother, I was found guilty
This time they threw the book at me
They also sang Please kill that child
They'll probably also sing Today, I'll die from starvation
I'm actually at the top of a planet that falls endlessly
I felt nauseous every day even when I lay down
Every day my hair got pulled into space and my feet floated up
My friend who lived without holding onto the wall left this planet first
Still, mold kept growing on my luggage that wanted to go somewhere
and sad winter rain came down all day
and unkempt graves were submerged under water every time it rained
In the end the birds that can only survive by landing
within the country's borders, a makeshift stage
all rotted and dropped dead
All night, in my dream, I fought with shit-water
that overflowed into my room

1. How the Last Words Looked

Everyone, please try to talk. Watch how speech disappears. Today's words walk away into the forest. They play a golden guitar, leaning against a worn-out wooden chair.

Feed the fire and try talking a bit. Know how to shout? Someone is erasing my words. Get erased, erased, newspaper bits are blowing about. Green, colored, star, crumbles. Golden notes fall out, and from somewhere a green snake appears and eats only the pauses. I'm out of breath. Out, of, breath…

Let's all laugh. I said laugh harder. We've at least got to laugh, don't we? Words are about to be erased together with the worn-out wooden chair. Sponge-like words crumble, leaving only a trace.

> Is it possible to love a sponge?
> Give the sponge some water.
> Temporary darkness—
> Continuation of the dark—
>
> Everyone say Ahh, open your mouths!

2. Anxiety of Words

Can you speak again? See how my green, green frozen words spin inside a basement cylinder press.

Talk with your mouth to the ground. Four-leafed clovers grow in successive patterns and time-flowers bloom as words. Talk with your mouth to the waves. Boats leave port and your words leap and rise as high as the gulls.

> Don't give any needles to our frozen words. Don't hide and watch where the words go after they get their shots.

> Suddenly a bell sounds—
> Cannon roars—

> Everyone say Ahh, open your mouths!

1

I decided to get an ultrasound of my whole body. I was hurting all over as if someone was orbiting the planetary system of my ribs. We are tired of hearing you say that you're sick, complained my family. Like planet Earth, someone was circling the sun, the sun that is so huge that no one can hear it scream as it burns. Perhaps a lethal virus has engulfed my body like the Milky Way? My body fluttered like a fish in an icebox. All my organs trembled as the technician pushed the camera against my body. Is this your first time? Turn sideways and roll over three times! the technician yelled. I saw planets with closed mouths that hid their long screams like padlocked freezers. The planet carried a schoolbag and took Line #4 to school to give a lecture and returned home on the same train—the planet's frozen face appeared then disappeared. The sun had a tight gravitational hold on Earth, not even a single drop of ocean escaped Earth. Every time I finished rotating, I saw myself inflating, filling the room even though I didn't explode. I couldn't move an inch as the place was completely filled with my body. I couldn't get up in the morning because I couldn't push myself away, I who weighed thousands of tons. Roll over three times and hold your breath! the technician yelled again.

2

(Like when the departing wind unlocks the window), he (like when he stands in the dark not knowing how to unlock the door), as soon as he (like when he tried to stop the fire from the mountains from coming in all by himself with his arms), and they (like when the headless dragonflies try to fly up), so she (like when a mosquito zigzags around you in the dark), and with the letter (like when the dusk quietly overtakes the burnt mountainside), then (like when he packs up and leave my body), and for a short time (like when I return to my empty house after being away for a couple of weeks and push aside the mail piled up in front of the door with my feet), for a long time (like when a burnt platanus tree keeps twisting itself to shake off the last leaf), to him (like when you blow air into the balloon with all your might only to have it burst), and keep calling him (like when the reservoir dries up, and leaves you a single sip of water), and after being dragged (like when the steam from deep inside the body is forced out) and at last (like when the night descends endlessly riding the burnt mountain), and then (like when you starve yourself for about ten days), finally (like when the room of air is tidied and a bouquet of roses scattered) No! How could you do this to me? (like when the tail end of the echo of the disappearing burnt mountain) ah ah ah ah, (like when you sweep everything off of the desk), but could you cut my story short and just give me my medicine?

3

Inside the palisade of ribs
the heart is well fed with blood
at the ranch of the heavenly universe
the sheep keeps feeding on grass
the hunting dogs called Time
growl outside the palisade
the quiet planets
can't even go beyond the fence
I am my prison
I am my prisoner
My eyes are my prison's guard posts
The pain that escapes the body
is no longer pain
but I still want to step outside
the ribs tonight

Asura, Yi Je-ha, Spring:
A ghost that enjoys fighting, Asura is a familiar figure in Buddhism. Yi Je-ha is a contemporary South Korean writer. In September 1996, a North Korean submarine broke down and landed on the east coast of South Korea. Eleven North Koreans were found dead on a nearby mountain. They had shot each other in an apparent suicide pact. In all 24 North Koreans were killed or found dead during the massive hunt carried out by South Korean troops. North Korea claimed that the submarine accidentally drifted into South Korea's waters, but South Korea maintained that the submarine was on a spying mission.

The Movie Our Descendants Most Hated:
Koreans use the English word "vocal" to refer to a singer in a band.

The Korean War began on June 25, 1950. Over four million people died in the war, which ended in 1953. North and South Korea still remain divided. May 18 refers to the Kwangju uprising of 1980 when, with the tacit consent of the U.S., South Korean troops massacred over 2000 civilians. The pro-democratic movement was protesting political and economic oppression under South Korea's military dictatorships.

Mommy Must be a Fountain of Feathers has been compiled from the following titles by Kim Hyesoon:

Tto tarŭn pyŏl esŏ. Seoul: Munhak kwa chisŏng sa, 1981.
Abŏjiga seun hŏsuabi. Seoul: Munhak kwa chisŏng sa, 1985.
Na ŭi up'anisyadŭ, Sŏul. Seoul: Munhak kwa chisŏng sa, 1994.
Pulssanghan sarang kigye. Seoul: Munhak kwa chisŏng sa, 1997.
Talyŏk kongjang kongjang jangnim poseyŏ. Seoul: Munhak kwa chisŏng sa, 2000.
Han chan ŭi pulgŭn kŏul. Seoul: Munhak kwa chisŏng sa, 2004.

Translator's Acknowledgements:
The translation of this project was supported by a generous grant from the Korea Literature Translation Institute (KLTI), Seoul.

Much gratitude to the editors of the following books and journals in which some of the translations first appeared: *Anxiety of Words: Contemporary Poetry by Korèan Women* (Zephyr Press, 2006), *When the Plug Gets Unplugged* (Tinfish Press, 2005), *Massachusetts Review, Action Yes, Fairy Tale Review, Sentence, Guernica* and *Azalea.*

I am most grateful to Joyelle McSweeney and Johannes Göransson for their persistent support and vision; Deborah Woodard for ongoing editorial feedback; Kim Hyesoon for her generosity in teaching me about Korean women's poetry and her trust in my translation; and Jay and Aaron for giving me a sense of home.

I dedicate this book to my niece and nephew, Na-Bi and Kyu-Jin, who were both born away from home.

KIM HYESOON (b. 1955) is a prominent South Korean poet. She began publishing in 1979 but only began to receive critical recognition almost two decades later. She has received numerous literary awards and was the first woman to receive the coveted Midang (2006) and Kim Su-yŏng (1998) awards named after two major contemporary poets. Midang was a poet who stood for *sunsusi* [pure poetry] while Kim Su-yŏng's poetry is closely associated with *ch'amyŏsi* [engaged poetry] that displays historical consciousness. Kim's poetry goes beyond the expectations of the established aesthetics and also *yŏryusi* [female poetry] which celebrates the passive, refined language. Kim lives in Seoul and teaches at Seoul Institute of the Arts.

DON MEE CHOI was born in South Korea and came to the states in 1981 to study art at Californian Institute of the Arts. After living in California and Arizona, she pursued her studies in contemporary Korean literature and translation. She now lives and works in Seattle. Her translations include *Anxiety of Words: Contemporary Poetry by Korean Women* (Zephyr, 2006) and *When the Plug Gets Unplugged* (Tinfish, 2005).

ACTION BOOKS CATALOG

2007 / 2008

WHIM MAN MAMMON
by Abraham Smith
ISBN 0-9765692-8-0
ISBN13: 978-0-9765692-8-2

THAUMATROPE
by Brent Hendricks
illustrations by
Lisa Hargon Smith
ISBN: 0-9765692-9-9
ISBN13: 978-0-9765692-9-9

PORT TRAKL
by Jaime Luis Huenún
translated by
Daniel Borzutzky
ISBN: 0-9799755-0-6
ISBN13: 978-0-9799755-0-9

MOMMY MUST BE
A FOUNTAIN OF FEATHERS
by Kim Hyesoon
translated by Don Mee Choi
ISBN: 0-9799755-1-4
ISBN13: 978-0-9799755-1-6

2006

YOU ARE A LITTLE BIT HAPPIER
THAN I AM
by Tao Lin
Winner of the 2005
December Prize
ISBN: 0-9765692-3-X
ISBN13: 978-0-9765692-3-7

YOU GO THE WORDS
by Gunnar Björling
translated by
Frederik Hertzberg
Scandinavian Series #2
ISBN: 0-9765692-5-6
ISBN13: 978-0-9765692-5-1

THE EDGE OF EUROPE
by Pentti Saarikoski
translated by Anselm Hollo
Scandinavian Series #3
ISBN: 0-9765692-6-4
ISBN13: 978-0-9765692-6-8

LOBO DE LABIO
by Laura Solórzano
translated by Jen Hofer
ISBN: 0-9765692-7-2
ISBN13: 978-0-9765692-7-5

2005

THE HOUNDS OF NO
by Lara Glenum
ISBN:0-97656592-1-3

MY KAFKA CENTURY
by Arielle Greenberg
ISBN:0-97656592-2-1

REMAINLAND:
SELECTED POEMS OF AASE BERG
by Aase Berg
translated by
Johannes Göransson
Scandinavian Series #1
ISBN:0-97656592-0-5